PUPIL DISCIPLINE AND EXCLUSIONS IN SCHOOLS

PUPIL DISCIPLINE AND EXCLUSIONS IN SCHOOLS

Bridget Lawson

Published by Longman Industry and Public Service Management, Longman Group UK Limited, 6th Floor, Westgate House, The High, Harlow, Essex CM20 1YR, England and Associated Companies throughout the world.
Telephone: Harlow (0279) 442601
Fax: Harlow (0279) 444501
Telex: 81491 Padlog

British Library Cataloguing in Publication Data
Lawson, Bridget
Pupil Discipline and Exclusions in Schools – (Longman/AGIT
  school governor training series).
  I. Title
  II. Series
  371.2

ISBN 0–582–08384–2

Phototypeset by Intype, London

Printed by Bell and Bain Ltd, Glasgow

Contents

Chapter 1
Introduction

Discipline in schools is as important to pupils' learning as any subject found in the formal curriculum. Schools are social institutions and one of their main purposes is to develop young people who are able to contribute to society while behaving in a way that is acceptable to society as a whole. Discipline and behavioural problems have been a subject of growing concern. Young people's attitudes to law and order; an increase in violent behaviour in society; a recognition of the extent of bullying in schools are some of the factors which contribute to this concern. There is an inevitable debate about whether the influence of teachers and school or the influence of parents and home is greater in the process of developing young people who need to understand and respect other people, their rights, and their property.

Home and school both contribute to the development of pupils' social skills. The kind of home circumstances and life experiences that pupils bring with them to school will affect the nature of their development. It will influence the formation of their values and whether these are generally agreed as acceptable. The school has a prescribed role to try to ensure that pupils ultimately fit into society as responsible adults. But sometimes home and school values will conflict. All schools will have built up ways of trying to perform their role using formal and informal systems. For example, school rules act as a formal mechanism for encouraging good behaviour, but how they are developed and applied can differ significantly from school to school. The involvement of governors in disciplinary issues will also vary depending on the philosophy and approach to such matters on the part of both Local Education Authorities (LEAs) and Headteachers.

Until recently there have been no legally defined rules to ensure consistency as to how pupils who seriously misbehave might be dealt with. The *Education (No 2) Act 1986* provides, for the first time, consistent procedures which identify certain responsibilities for governors, headteachers and LEAs in dealing with disciplinary issues.

The 1986 Act began to extend the management responsibilities of governors and these are more clearly defined in the *Education Reform Act 1988*. Governors now have a legal duty to ensure that discipline issues are managed effectively within their school, as well as specific responsibilities in relation to exclusion procedures. (Exclusion occurs when a pupil is not allowed to attend school for a defined or undefined period, or ever again.)

While it is important to have procedures which try to achieve consistency of approach between schools, there are many complex factors to take into account when dealing with extreme cases of indiscipline. Different people will be involved, who may have a direct or indirect link with the school. Parents or guardians play an extremely important part and their involvement and participation is needed. There is a network of support agencies which may become involved and governors need to be aware of these.

Pupil discipline should not be viewed only in the context of rules and punishments. Although the focus of this book is on discipline and exclusions, rewards for success are just as important, which means valuing the achievements of individual pupils, as well as those resulting from the collective efforts of the whole school. A school discipline policy should include systems and procedures for both rewards and punishments.

Pupil Discipline and Exclusions in Schools has been written primarily for school governors. It describes their legal responsibilities in the exclusion process, and aims to help them to consider exclusions within the broader context of pupil discipline issues. It should help governors to make responsible and informed decisions which may well have a significant effect on a young person's life. The legal aspects are complex, involving different parties whose responsibilities overlap. For this reason some of the information given in the text may seem repetitive. This is necessary to clarify the various roles and responsibilities of the parties involved.

While exclusions, especially permanent exclusions, are much more likely to occur in the secondary sector, issues of discipline are just as important in primary education. Extremely disruptive behaviour may be more manageable with younger children because infant and primary schools are smaller than secondary schools and because younger children are more likely to respond to adults. Class teachers, therefore, are likely to have more opportunity to develop a relationship with each child. Provided that the relationship is a sound one, the teacher can pick up problems of individuals and groups of children in their early stages. This is not, unfortunately, always the case. Where serious discipline problems do occur, the facilities for helping the younger disruptive child are often scarcer than those which exist for older children. While many references and examples which follow relate more specifically to older pupils, this does not mean that the same principles do not apply to younger children.

The book comprises three sections. Chapters 2–5 consider pupil discipline, first within the school and then from a wider perspective. This provides the context in which the legislative issues need to be viewed. Chapters 6–8 cover the legal framework which relates to pupil exclusions. The final part of the book contains six case studies.

Notes

1. Section 22 of the 1986 Act relates principally to matters of discipline. Sections 23–25 set out the procedures dealing with exclusions and Sections 26 and 27 are concerned with appeals. Guidance on their implementation is given in *Circular 7/87, Education (No 2) Act: Further Guidance*. These sections of the Act are reproduced in Appendix 1.

2. Arrangements for dealing with some of the procedures in relation to pupil exclusions and discipline are different in voluntary aided and special agreement schools. The relevant differences are noted as they occur.

Chapter 2
Pupil discipline in schools

Key points

- School context
- Pastoral care and other support
- Special educational needs

School context

Discipline is about behaviour and everyone has her or his own views and opinions as to what constitutes reasonable behaviour. This means that there is likely to be argument about what types of behaviour should or should not be tolerated in schools. All parties involved – staff, pupils, parents and governors – must try to work together to achieve some consensus. They all will need to contribute to ensuring that school rules help the school to function effectively so that development occurs within a framework of order and control.

There is a continuum of different behaviours with which anyone working in a school needs to be able to cope. Unacceptable behaviour may include pupils in classrooms who inhibit or prevent other pupils from learning. Such behaviour could take the form of constant chatter, abusive language to a teacher or other pupils, or physical assault on other pupils or staff. All of these are potentially disruptive to the learning process and may also present a safety hazard to others. Clearly they do not all warrant the same sort of punishment, but there is a need to deal with the disruptions. Fiddling around in the classroom may not sound like disruptive behaviour, but at what point might it become so? The school playground is a place for pupils to socialise, relax, 'let off steam', between lessons. Some pupils, though, dread 'playtime' because they fear the behaviour of gangs and bullies, and the occupation of large areas of space by dominant groups.

Many people do not like some rules. Some do not like any. The validity of rules is always tested. But some rules may be more appropriate than many may think. That does not mean that there are not examples which at best can be described as silly! It is not surprising, therefore, that rules are queried and not always understood.

This is likely to be particularly true of pupils, whatever their age. They often cannot see the point of what they are being told to do, or not to do. Parents, teachers, governors, and the community at large might recognise that some rules are essential for the effective operation of a school. Pupils will not necessarily think so. A major issue about discipline in schools is trying to persuade pupils about the validity of the reasons for rules or, by the carrot and stick method, trying to ensure that they are all obeyed regardless. This reinforces the need for clearly stated discipline policies that include the school rules and penalties for breaking them which are known about and understood. This helps to ensure a consistent and appropriate use of penalties within a system which is seen and judged to be fair, if not necessarily liked!

Some schools value the contribution that pupils make to a school's behaviour policy or code of practice and involve them in the process. Evidence submitted to the Elton Report (1989) *Discipline in Schools* suggested that schools can promote better behaviour among their pupils by giving them more responsibilities. The report recommends that pupils should be given every opportunity to take responsibilities and to make a full contribution to improving behaviour in schools. The *Education (No 2) Act 1986* ended the choice of allowing pupils to be members of governing bodies, but some secondary schools have school councils which act as a forum for discussion between pupils and teachers. These provide an opportunity for open discussion about school matters to which pupils can contribute. Although this sort of arrangement is more likely to be set up formally in the secondary sector, all pupils can provide information about the school as seen from their perspective. This can help to shape behaviour policies to which all involved parties are more likely to have ownership and commitment.

While teachers are expected to handle discipline as part of their day to day work, the headteacher has overall responsibility for the internal

organisation and management of the school. The way that discipline
issues are dealt with in practice will be influenced to a great extent by
the head's leadership and management style. If governors are to be able
to make sensible and fair judgements about pupil sanctions and
behaviour they must know enough about what is going on in the school
as a whole; how the school rules are drawn up and applied; how they
support the school's policy statement on discipline; and how the rules
reinforce what the school stands for in its published statement of aims
and purpose. Governors' responsibilities in relation to discipline are
therefore linked to all their other responsibilities. The Elton Report
(1989) stated that 'the behaviour of pupils in a school is influenced by
almost every aspect of the way in which it is run and how it relates to
the community it serves. It is the combination of all these factors which
gives a school its character and identity.'

Pastoral care and other support

In schools the term *pastoral* usually relates to a combination of the
academic, welfare and discipline activities. In primary schools the class
teacher plays a key role. In secondary schools there is usually a more
extensive pastoral system. This will probably include a pupil's form
tutor, as well as senior pastoral staff such as heads of year or house.

Heads of department may also take on some responsibility for
behavioural matters and communicate information as necessary to the
pastoral team. A deputy head is likely to have overall responsibility for
ensuring that the agreed discipline and welfare systems are carried out
appropriately in the school.

Each school will develop its own particular way of doing things.
However senior staff with pastoral responsibilities will normally be
expected to give advice and support to their teacher colleagues, as well
as deal with pupil behaviour problems that have gone beyond the scope
of the classroom, tutor group teacher or departmental head. All involved
must keep accurate and confidential records. The pastoral team should
be in a position to monitor events through the agreed reporting and
recording systems, and to identify behaviour patterns in the school.
Governors should receive regular reports on this aspect of a school.

The LEA also provides additional support, for example, from the
education welfare service, educational psychology service, and teacher

support and multicultural education support units. Once again, the organisation of these services varies from LEA to LEA. They may be centrally, regionally, or school-based. Their future administration may well change as Local Management of Schools (LMS) develops. Other examples of the available network of support to schools include social services and the police. In some schools support from religious leaders will be particularly important.

While governors must expect and allow professional staff to pursue the work they are employed to do, they can also expect to be assured that the systems and networks of support are working together and that there is communication between them. Governors will also need to be confident that teachers are using tutorial and pastoral time as effectively as possible and that staff have the necessary skills to deal with behaviour problems. Part of the governors' role is to ask questions about how the system is working, and if any parts of the system are not working, to find out where there is a weak link. Heads and pastoral teams should not feel defensive about critical questioning and about being asked to provide information. Governors will be failing in their duty if they are not prepared to ask questions and to recommend appropriate action. This is part of the process of evaluation, the results of which should feed in to the school planning process.

Special educational needs

The main focus of this section is *not* on pupils who have a *Statement of Special Educational Need*, that is, children with needs associated with particular learning difficulties which call for the LEA to determine special educational provision. It concentrates on the many children who, at some time or another during their time at school, are in need of help over and above what is provided as the norm. In the *Warnock Report* of *1978* it was estimated that, at any given time, approximately 20 per cent of pupils have special educational needs. Only about two per cent of the total school population have statements.

Special educational needs for which no statement is relevant may arise for many different reasons. For example, a pupil might be ill for a long period of time and need extra help with their studies.

He or she might suffer some emotional disturbance such as disharmony at home, or the death of a close relative or friend. The causes are often not easy to see or discover but the effects can be traumatic. Special needs of this sort may result in a conflict between the pupil and the authority of the school because the pupil is struggling to learn, feels at odds with the learning environment, and demands special help by behaving in an attention-seeking way. Emotional and behavioural difficulties often lead to discipline problems, and schools need to be able to address special needs of this sort, whether or not the need resulted from a situation within the home or the school.

Providing adequate support for pupils in mainstream schools who have special educational needs of any sort has been a source of concern for many years. This concern has been aggravated by both formula funding and the demands of the national curriculum.

The number of pupils who might have special needs in the future is difficult to project, and apportioning scarce resources accurately to support pupils with special needs is therefore difficult. LEAs have to make decisions about the distribution of resources as efficiently as possible. Allocating funds to meet a moving target such as the number of pupils likely to have special needs in any school at any one time, is not the sort of neat and tidy situation which policymakers like, because figures cannot be calculated on the basis of known numbers. Support for special needs continues to remain a low priority in terms of LEA spending. It is not helped by the regulations which govern how funds should be allocated to schools through formula funding. These do not allow LEAs to submit proposals which necessarily take into account all the various issues which need to be identified in relation to special education in mainstream schools. In LEAs where special educational needs are given a high priority, governors in schools with delegated budgets will still need to decide how the school budget should be spent.

All pupils share the same statutory rights to a broad and balanced curriculum, including access to the national curriculum. Governors have a responsibility to ensure that this obligation is met. The statutory requirements of the national curriculum can be adapted to take account of groups or individual pupils with a particular kind of special need. However, governors will need to assure themselves that in the event of an adaptation being proposed, the reason does not relate to insufficient or inappropriate staffing. This is particularly important when they are assessing whether there is adequate support for special needs within the school as a whole.

Governors in schools with a delegated budget will need to be aware of the resource implications for their school when planning their budgets and about the freedom they have to reconsider spending priorities. They also have specific legal responsibilities in relation to special educational needs. Under the *Education Reform Act 1988* the basic responsibility of governing bodies for arrangements for special educational needs in mainstream schools is to identify, assess and meet the special educational needs of children who do not require a formal Statement of Needs although this will normally be done through the headteacher. This further endorses the responsibilities given to governors in *Section 2(5) of the 1981 Education Act,* which states that:

It shall be the duty of the governors, in the case of a county or voluntary school, and of the local education authority by whom the school is maintained, in the case of a maintained nursery school:

(a) To use their best endeavours, in exercising their functions in relation to the school, to secure that if any registered pupil has special educational needs the special educational provision that is required for him is made;

(b) To secure that, where the responsible person has been informed by the local education authority that a registered pupil has special educational needs, those needs are made known to all who are likely to teach him; and

(c) To secure that the teachers in the school are aware of the importance of identifying, and providing for, those registered pupils who have specal educational needs.

Legislation still refers to he/him when it means he/she or him/her.

The arrangements for excluding a pupil from a special school are the same as for those in mainstream education. In addition to the specific physical, emotional or other learning difficulties of the pupils often there are other differences for those in special schools. For example, pupils are often placed outside their own catchment areas or their own LEA's geographical boundary. This can make community involvement difficult or impossible.

Chapter 3

Pupil discipline — a wider perspective

Key points

- The school in the community
- Parents
- Parent governors

The school in the community

Each school is a separate community but is also part of a wider community within its own geographical location. The relationship between a school and its wider community is important, otherwise schools may become isolated from the world outside and from the cultures and values which influence their pupils. Schools can positively promote community involvement, for example, through, provision of adult learning, community education programmes which meet the educational, social and recreational needs of community residents. The changes to the membership of governing bodies to include more parent and community representatives (*Sections 3–5 Education (No 2) Act 1986*) have encouraged greater involvement of local communities in school matters. Powers of cooption should be used with care to ensure that there is adequate and appropriate representation on the governing body from the school's local community.

Contributions from the local business people, voluntary groups, and the police to practical projects as well as personal and social education programmes, together with liaison with education welfare officers to reduce instances of truancy, are other examples of how schools can work more closely with the community and make a positive contribution to improving standards of behaviour. Members of the community usually first judge the school on how its pupils behave: for example, the extent of truancy and vandalism.

Parents can choose to send their child to any school of their choice provided there are places available. Most choose their local school. Hopefully this is because they feel confident in the school because the teachers, governors, and all associated with it have recognised that it is an important part of the community. To achieve this, school contact with parents and guardians of pupils and/or potential pupils is needed.

Schools are required to provide information on a range of aspects: much may be included in the school prospectus, and must include details of the disciplinary procedures used in the school. The school prospectus is a document which communicates information about the school to the world outside. It is an opportunity to let the community know about the school, what it does, how it operates, about relations between staff and pupils, the school and parents, the school and the community at large. Better still, if parents and others are able to build upon this written information through firsthand knowledge gained by visiting the school and talking with staff and pupils. Many schools work hard and successfully at promoting home, school, and community links, for example, through parent and parent–teacher associations. Governors may take the opportunity to attend open evenings and parents' evenings to talk with parents and prospective parents. Many primary schools actively involve parents through working in the classroom and in home-learning schemes. Some schools have a community room, or have set aside an area for parents and governors. Developing access like this illustrates a positive attitude to opening up the school to the world outside. Arguments which are used to discourage these sorts of initiatives, for example lack of time or available space, should be questioned rather than accepted at face value. They may be justified, but such contributions often come from people with closed minds and can be powerful influences against trying out new ideas.

Schools which are designated community schools or colleges already have an established community link, but this may not necessarily include the majority of parents. Governors need to know what schemes exist in their school to encourage parent and community partnerships, and who holds responsibility for developing them. Many governing bodies have established subcommittees which include parent–community liaison within their areas of responsibility, and teachers participate in their membership.

Schools want to create a good impression. Enabling and encouraging the local community to know what the school is like can help to achieve this. There is a need for a mutual set of expectations which will help to establish a means of agreement between parents, teachers, and the community as a whole, as to what the school is about, and in this context — how its pupils can be expected to behave. Secondary schools must recognise the importance of feeder primary schools as a vital part of their wider community. Closer liaison between the secondary and primary sectors may help to increase the chances of young pupils with behaviour problems to succeed in their new environment. This is likely to be more successful if strategies have been developed to support these pupils in advance of their transfer from primary to secondary school.

Parents

The previous section emphasised the need for schools to develop positive and strong links with their communities, a key part to this process being the parents. If things start to go wrong for a pupil and their parents are familiar enough with the way the school works, they are more likely to be willing to come in to the school to try and sort things out.

Schools have not always been the most welcoming of places to parents. Some parents are seen as very difficult visitors. While they are, inevitably, partners in the home–school relationship, this does not mean that they necessarily feel comfortable in the school setting, particularly if they are not encouraged to feel so.

Parents are not always aware of how their children behave at school. If they are asked to visit the school about a discipline matter, they may in fact be surprised, even embarrassed. Should it get to the point of involving others, for example, the education welfare service, there is no reason to assume that parents will easily welcome, or be able to cope with this. The situation may be anxious and stressful for them, particularly if they are wanting to cooperate but find it difficult to know how to do so. Developing good relationships with parents is not always easy but needs to be accepted as part of the school's total communication process. Schools should be welcoming places and any information given to parents, whether written or spoken, should be clear and comprehensive. In some areas it would be good practice to translate information into predominant community languages.

One of the findings of the Mortimore *et al. School Matters* study of junior schools published in 1988 was that school effectiveness is related to parental involvement. The most effective junior schools in the sample, in terms of work, behaviour and attendance, were those which had the best informal relationships with parents. These schools encouraged parental involvement in a variety of ways.

Any serious instance of pupil disciplinary problems within the school should involve contact with parents or guardians of the pupil(s) at the earliest possible opportunity. There is evidence to show that the success or failure of attempts to deal with *problem* pupils depends heavily on the quality of parental response, which often depends on the school's attitude towards parents. A report *Bedfordshire High and Upper Schools Responses to Difficult and Disruptive Behaviour* produced in 1988–89 found that:

Just as the nature of the relationship between teacher and pupil seemed a crucial one so did that between teacher and parent. Schools which encouraged easy and open contact and conveyed positive news of pupils as enthusiastically as accounts of misdemeanour seemed to fare better in the response they received when trouble loomed . . .

There are many ways in which schools can, and do, involve parents in their work. Governors should recognise their role in being a necessary and active link between the school and its community. They should understand and critically examine the systems the school has in place, to try to ensure that good channels of two-way communication between the school, parents and the wider community exist, particularly as an aid to promoting good behaviour. When a pupil is excluded from school it is usually as a result of serious or persistent misbehaviour. Their readmission to school is not necessarily an easy or smooth process. It requires understanding and agreement about what is required of the pupil and of his or her parents/guardians. This reinforces the need for good channels of two-way communication as referred to above. The Elton Report (1989) recommended that 'headteachers should use reentry agreements, specifying the conditions under which an excluded pupil can be readmitted to school, as a means of ending indefinite exclusions'. This could also apply to pupils who are reinstated after being permanently excluded. (Reinstatement is considered in more detail in Chapter 8.) This approach requires a relationship which contains at least an element of trust between the pupil, the parents, and the school. Parents do not necessarily respond positively to conditions being applied as a prerequisite for their child being allowed to return to school. Governors may need to be aware of difficulties which may face the school from parents/guardians who for whatever reason, refuse to have anything to do with the discipline of their child, including the exclusion process.

Parent governors

These are often the governors closest to the school. The majority have a child or children in the school and they are in a position to receive firsthand information about what goes on. For example, notes and letters to parents from the form or head teacher, and telling of 'what I've done', or 'what happened today' from their children. The accuracy of this reporting cannot always be guaranteed, but access to this sort of firsthand information can be very useful. Perhaps with the exception of the chair of governors, who may ask to receive copies of all communications sent to parents from the school as a matter of course, this information is not likely to be available to most other governors. Parent governors are also likely to have more opportunities to visit the school because of their children. Also they are more likely to talk with other parents and thus acquire a broader perspective about how things seem.

This access to information can be very useful, but must be used wisely. For example, a parent may come first to a parent governor, especially if they know them, to talk about a discipline problem. Should this happen it is very important that the parent governor does not become involved in gossip. There are, or should be, established lines of communication for dealing with school issues. For example, if a mother is concerned about her child's progress in mathematics, her initial action should be to see the child's class teacher or form tutor. If a parent governor is stopped in the street by a parent who complains that his/her child has been 'thrown out of school', what should be the response?

A governor should always exercise caution in what he or she says in a situation like this. It is important to follow the procedure agreed by the school and the governing body on discipline matters. It would be unwise to become involved in detailed discussion without first referring the matter to the headteacher and the chair of governors. This will help to ensure that consistent information is given by all involved parties at all times. It should also reinforce the importance of treating all discipline matters in confidence.

Chapter 4

Discipline issues

Key points

- What is misbehaviour?
- Dealing with misbehaviour
- Policies and codes of practice

What is misbehaviour?

All pupils are likely to misbehave sometimes. Part of their learning about life is trying things out, seeing how far they can go, and taking risks. Generally such behaviour does not give cause for worry or concern. Teachers deal with it in their stride as it arises.

Situations in which pupils consistently refuse to cooperate with staff and/or demonstrate behaviour which shows no respect for others or for themselves, usually require handling in a different way. Examples of this include petty or major theft and crime, using abusive language, truanting, bullying and racial or sexual harassment.

Recent research suggests that bullying is a lot more prevalent in schools than had hitherto been thought. Often both bullies and their victims are unpopular with their peers. Schools must take some action in such situations because unpopular children frequently develop adjustment problems, leading to delinquency or dropping out. In their booklet *Bullying: A Positive Response — Advice for parents, governors and staff in schools* Delwyn Tattum and Graham Herbert state the following:

Sadly, bullying is a form of cruelty which is widely practised in our schools and yet it has received little attention from national and local authorities. Nonetheless, most who work in education will agree that it is widespread and persistent.

Schools have a responsibility to create a secure and safe environment for pupils who are in their care so that parents may send their children to school in the confident knowledge that they will be protected from bullies.

Bullying can take the form of both physical and verbal abuse, including racial and sexual harassment. Name-calling, racial insults, offensive graffiti, are some examples. It is important that teachers form good role models for pupils and that their language and behaviour is fair and consistent to all the people with whom they deal. Governors can find out very quickly what sort of atmosphere exists in the school and whether all children are tolerated regardless of their sex, race and colour. If they keep their eyes and ears alert on every visit to the school an observant governor will pick up clues as to how things are. For example, how pupils relate to each other and to staff; whether swearing, rudeness to adults or taunting of peers goes unchecked, or if there is evidence of graffiti, or litter. Such signs give an indication about the way in which the school's behaviour policy is being carried out either positively or negatively.

Pupils are not the only ones who need protection in schools. Teachers need protection too. There is growing concern about the number of assaults on teachers by pupils. The *British Crime Survey 1988* found that teachers are three times more likely to be threatened than people in most other occupations. From detailed analysis of questionnaires completed by teachers about the incidence of physical aggression by pupils towards teachers, the *Elton Report* stated that their 'best estimate is that about one in two hundred (0.5 per cent) teachers had had experiences of this kind'. Guidelines have now been produced by the Health and Safety Commission to help schools and local authorities tackle this problem. Their recommendations include the entitlement to counselling, time off, and legal advice for teachers who are attacked by pupils or parents. Governors need to be aware of the resource implications as well as the human issues related to discipline situations of this kind.

Dealing with misbehaviour

School rules and disciplinary measures should be clearly stated. All pupils should be aware of them and understand them. Each school will have its own way of sanctioning pupils for different breaches of discipline. An important aspect of this is how sanctions are applied and the processes involved. This is heavily dependent on the quality of relationship that teachers have with pupils. For example, a school may have a reputation about the excellent behaviour of its pupils. This could be achieved by adopting a strict, authoritarian approach to teacher–pupil relationships, or through a more relaxed process. Each person's preferences as a teacher or pupil will be influenced by a range of different factors, including their own childhood experiences. What works for one person may well not work for another.

Drawing on research conducted by David Reynolds and others in South Wales, and by Michael Rutter and his team in inner London, Martin Rosenbaum concludes that:

Schools which are positive and tolerant rather than authoritarian and punitive tend to be better at preventing disruption, and that pupils' behaviour usually is better when schools:

Treat pupils fairly and with respect;
Strive to build cooperative rather than antagonistic teacher–pupil relationships;
Do not impose petty and unnecessary rules;
Are quick to reward and slow to punish;
Give pupils responsibility and rights to active participation;
Exhibit concern for pupils' welfare and responsiveness to their needs;
Ensure that teachers provide good models of behaviour.

Schools use a variety of sanctions ranging from a spontaneous telling-off; detention; putting pupils on report; to an exclusion of some kind. The behaviour of any child is seldom consistent and a pupil may be the model of good behaviour one day and quite the opposite the next! In the vast majority of cases behaviour problems can be sorted out without resorting to the exclusion process.

Issues about school discipline are very complex. Governors need to be aware of how the school acts about discipline in general as well as about extreme problems. They need to be confident that discipline issues are handled in a sensitive and caring way with positive results.

The aim must always be to resolve a problem in the most helpful way, rather than giving a punishment for its own sake.

Policies and codes of practice

There is clearly a difference between what governors must do to comply with the law, and what they may choose to do to supplement their legal responsibilities. Discipline policies that have been provided by LEAs should have untangled some of the more complicated legal jargon but will be general in terms. Governors will need to ensure that their own school policy is not only correct in law but also relates specifically to their school's aims, goals, and values. The approach that is being used to do this by some schools is to extend a discipline and exclusion policy to a whole school behaviour policy. Such a policy incorporates other areas which have been highlighted by many LEAs — for example:

> Equal opportunities, which relate to race, gender and special educational needs;
> Insurance, which includes protection to teachers, other members of staff and governors;
> Playtime and playground activities (particularly for the primary sector);
> Recruitment and selection of staff which include criteria to ensure, as nearly as possible, the appointment of candidates with appropriate discipline skills as well as subject knowledge.

Codes of conduct may also form part of a school's behaviour policy and relate to a range of different aspects of school life. Such practice helps to clarify expectations on the part of both pupils and teachers. Governors need to be aware of the interrelationship between the school's discipline and exclusion policy, agreed codes of conduct, and a whole school behaviour policy if there is one.

Chapter 5

The effective governing body

Key points

- **Roles**
- **Responsibilities**
- **Ways of organising**

Roles

Governors have a role to ensure that policies and procedures in the school are carried out in a just and fair way. Part of this will relate to how discipline is exercised within the school as a whole, and part will relate specifically to the exclusion process laid down by law. The involvement of individual governors will vary depending on how each governing body is organised.

Governors should not be involved in the day-to-day running of the school. They bring an outside perspective to school situations enabling them to stand back from the closer involvement of those who work in the school. This does not mean that their involvement in supporting, or not supporting, a decision by the headteacher in respect of punishing a pupil is easy. In any situation every person carries their own views, attitudes, and prejudices. Governors must be willing and able to take as objective a view as is possible about any facts put before them. They should not be expected, or expect to support decisions which relate to pupil discipline or exclusions if they do not have prior knowledge about a situation in which they become involved. Governors may feel a conflict between the need to care for children and the need to support the headteacher and school staff. They may feel they should be loyal to the headteacher above all else. They may feel that they need to react to pressure from parents, particularly if they are parent governors, to take a different view from that put forward by the school. They may feel let down if the LEA rules against their decision.

These sorts of pressures can be reduced if those involved are clear about their different roles. This will help the development of an effective working partnership.

Responsibilities

Governors are responsible for the overall management of the school. They are accountable for this management to pupils, parents, teachers and to the community as a whole. Some are elected, some are appointed and others are coopted. Being accountable, they therefore all share the responsibility with teachers for discipline in the school. Through the previous chapters it should be clear that it is an area of extreme complexity and diversity involving lay people from the community (not only governors) as well as highly trained professionals. Ideally every young person would attend a school which provided the best possible fit for him or her in terms of learning opportunities, resources, development of potential. At the moment this is far from being a reality for most children in this country. Schools can only do so much, especially within resource constraints. Some seem to do better than others. Some will seldom, if ever, exclude or permanently exclude a pupil. This is not necessarily a good thing, it could be an indicator of weak or inappropriate management. Judging the overall performance of a school will mean assessing many interlinked factors. Governors have the right as well as the duty to question as well as to support the actions of all those involved in the management of the school.

Policies need to be monitored and reviewed regularly and governors, through *Section 32 of the 1986 Act*, have the right to ask the headteacher for reports on any aspect of his or her duties. This should include regular reports on standards of behaviour, attendance levels and any other aspect of pupil discipline that governors may decide they need or want to know about. In their turn, governors should keep parents informed on these matters, for example, through the minutes of governors' meetings, newsletters, and the governors' annual report to parents.

Ways of organising

Chapter 6 outlines the specific responsibilities of the headteacher, the LEA and the governing body in cases of exclusion. Bearing in mind that governors are usually willing volunteers and that many have time constraints, it is not unusual for specific duties to be allocated to individuals or subgroups of the main governing body, for example, a pastoral team, or subcommittee. The chairperson can decide whether he or she wishes to be a member of that committee, which might include in its membership teachers with pastoral responsibilities.

Generally it is not necessary or appropriate for the whole governing body to be kept informed of day-to-day disciplinary issues. This point is considered in more detail in Chapter 7 in relation to the exclusion process. Governors who are members of a pastoral–discipline subcommittee will be informed about pupils who are causing concern. The headteacher should keep the chair of governors informed of matters of concern, although he or she might be a member of that subcommittee.

There are other ways in which governors can help. For example, they can bring an external perspective to situations which have become very close to some teachers and to the pastoral team. This might include using them as a sounding board for different ways of approaching a difficult problem, or seeking their views, for example, on the tone or content of a letter to a parent. One of the strengths of a shared approach is the opportunity to pool ideas. This can often result in the creation of new and better ones. This requires, of course, a close and trusting partnership between governors, teachers and the head.

Giving parents formal rights to question a headteacher's decision to exclude their child introduces a more democratic approach to pupil punishment. Parents can be helped or hindered in using this right, for example, by the way in which information is communicated to them. Governors should be aware of the content of letters sent to parents informing them of a pupil exclusion, and of their right of appeal if they wish to do so. Governors should also be satisfied that parents and pupils know that they can raise any concerns they may have about discipline issues and that they know how to do so. Having a set of procedures, or a *communications code of practice* for parents which clearly sets out the process agreed by the school and the governors, can help to remove any confusion or uncertainty that may exist. The information could be included in the school prospectus or produced as a separate document. A *communications code of practice* could include and expand on the more formal arrangements for school visits by parents which exist, such as parents' evenings. It might also contain a summary of all the processes used to communicate with parents, the purposes of the communication, how often each occurs (including the school's boundaries or otherwise on open access), and who is involved. Details of discipline policy issues could be contained within this, for example, when letters are sent relating to detentions and exclusions, as well as praise for good work.

Chapter 6

Pupil exclusions — the legal framework

Key points

- **Types of exclusion**
- **Duties and responsibilities of:**
  Governors
  Headteachers
  Local Education Authority (LEA)

Types of exclusion

The term *exclusion* as defined in the *Education (No 2) Act 1986* covers any instance in which a pupil is punished by being kept away from school by order of the headteacher. Exclusions are the maximum disciplinary sanction available following the prohibition of corporal punishment, and there are three kinds of exclusion:

1. **Fixed** exclusion — when the pupil's date of return is determined in advance of the exclusion, and the parent(s)/guardian (or the pupil if he or she is aged 18 or over) is told in advance of the reason for the exclusion and the date on which he or she is expected to return. The pupil must return on this date even if any other conditions, such as a planned meeting between the parents and the headteacher, has not taken place. A fixed period of exclusion may be succeeded by a further fixed exclusion at any time.

2. **Indefinite** exclusion — when no date of return is decided. This might occur, for example, when a condition is set such as a meeting between parents and the headteacher, or when medical advice is being taken.

3. **Permanent** exclusion — when a pupil is not allowed to return to the school. The headteacher can at any point decide that a fixed period or indefinite exclusion will be made permanent.

In voluntary aided and special agreement schools the procedures relating to permanent exclusion are slightly different. This is explained in more detail in Appendix 1.

Only the headteacher can exclude a pupil from a county, voluntary controlled or maintained special school — although governors, the Local Education Authority (LEA) and parents have responsibilities and rights in relation to the process.

The responsibilities and duties of the governors, the headteacher and the LEA are outlined below.

Duties and responsibilities

Governors

Governors have the right to provide a written statement of general principles on discipline matters which may include exclusions. Also they may offer guidance to the head on particular aspects of school discipline, such as acceptable standards of behaviour, which the head should take into account when developing the disciplinary side of school management with his or her staff. The majority of LEAs will have provided schools with guidance on discipline policies. Such document-ation may be sufficient to satisfy the law that a school discipline policy has been produced. It is good practice, however, for governing bodies to ensure that such guidance is adapted to meet the particular needs, culture, and ethos of their school.

Governors must be informed by the headteacher of any exclusion which will cause any pupil to have been excluded for a total of five days or more in any one term, or which will cause the pupil to miss the opportunity of taking a public examination. Governors may confirm or change the duration of an exclusion if it is fixed. If it is indeterminate they may decide a date for the readmission of the pupil.

Parents have the right to query the appropriateness of any exclusion with the governing body. The governors must consider any representations from parents and decide whether to confirm or modify the headteacher's decision.

The LEA must consult the governors should the authority wish to reinstate a pupil whom the governors have agreed should be excluded permanently or for a fixed period.

The governors must comply with any directive the LEA makes after such consultation; but in the case of permanent exclusions they may appeal against a directive to reinstate a pupil which has been given by the LEA. All decisions of Appeals Panels are final and binding.

Headteachers

The overall responsibility for ensuring good discipline in the school is that of the headteacher, aided by his or her staff. They must determine and publish within the school measures which promote good conduct (including rules and provisions for their enforcement), in accordance with the principles agreed by the governors. Headteachers have specific duties, powers and responsibilities in relation to the exclusion process. Only they have the power to exclude a pupil.

Headteachers must inform the parents of any exclusion as soon as a decision to exclude has been made. They must give the reasons for the exclusion, state the type, and the date the exclusion will end. They must also inform the parents that they have a right to make representations to the governors and/or the LEA. They must also inform the governors of any exclusion as described above. If a temporary exclusion is made permanent, the headteacher must inform the parents, the governors and the LEA. In the case of permanent exclusions, all parents can appeal to an independent panel (through the LEA), once all other options have been exhausted.

Headteachers must comply with any directive given by the governors or the LEA (as appropriate) but have the option of making an indefinite exclusion permanent. The headteacher has the authority to do this when the LEA has overruled a decision of the governors not to reinstate.

Headteachers must comply with any final decision arrived at by the LEA or an Appeals Panel (subject to the governors' right of appeal against an LEA decision).

Local Education Authority (LEA)

The LEA must decide whether pupils permanently excluded should be reinstated but must consult the governors first.

The LEA may give directions regarding the reinstatement of a pupil excluded for a fixed period, including overruling a decision of the governors not to reinstate, or reducing the period of exclusion, but, again, they must consult the governors first.

The LEA must arrange for the hearing of appeals submitted by either governors or parents or both, and must inform all parties of the outcome.

The LEA must set out the statutory requirements in the *Articles of Government* of maintained schools, including any additional appeals procedures. All governors should receive a copy of the *Articles of Government* from the LEA as of right.

Each one of the three parties must communicate decisions within the power and authority that each has, to the other two.

LEA's reserve powers

In a county, controlled or maintained special school, the LEA can take any necessary steps to prevent a breakdown of discipline caused either by the behaviour of pupils, or by any action taken by pupils at the school. Should this situation arise in aided or special agreement schools, the governors and head must consider any representation by the LEA. (*Section 28 of the 1986 Act*).

This summary describes the key areas of responsibility of each of the parties involved. It is complicated and governors can expect to rely on the advice and support of LEA personnel. It is also important to remember that the vast majority of exclusions are for a fixed period, affect a small minority of pupils, and are mostly unchallenged by governors or parents. This does not mean, however, that any exclusion should be treated lightly.

B

Chapter 7

The exclusion process

Key points

- **Steps and stages**
- **Involvement of governors**
- **Record-keeping**

Steps and stages

A variety of sanctions will be used in schools and how pupils are punished should depend on the nature of their misbehaviour. Exclusions are a serious form of punishment, not least because they ban a pupil from school premises, which under most other circumstances is against the law. The use of exclusions must, therefore, fit in with the range of other punitive measures used in the school, but should be used only for misdemeanours which are rated as particularly serious. Most exclusions will have been preceded by informal discussions between the headteacher, the parents, and probably LEA support services.

Involvement of governors

Any serious instance of pupil disciplinary problems within the school should involve contact with the parents or guardians of the pupil(s) at the earliest possible opportunity. Governors may be involved informally at this stage, but have no legally required involvement until a pupil is excluded and at that point the governors have certain specific obligations:

1. They must receive any comments from parents (or pupils if aged 18 or over) that they may want to make about any type of exclusion.

2. They must be prepared to either confirm any exclusion which amounts to over five days in aggregate in any term; or one where an opportunity to complete essential examination coursework or to take a public examination would be lost; or to order reinstatement.

3. They must consider any indefinite exclusion and either order reinstatement immediately or by a set date, or endorse the headteacher's action and ensure that the LEA is informed.

4. They must consider whether to make a formal appeal against any order of the LEA for the reinstatement of a pupil who has been permanently excluded.

Governors need to agree their own procedures for dealing with different aspects of the exclusion process so that they are prepared to respond quickly and effectively to any exclusion case. Decisions could be taken by the whole body, delegated to the chair, or to the chair in consultation with, for example, members of the pastoral–discipline subcommittee of the governing body (if there is one). Delegation has advantages in that it enables decisions to be made quickly and circumvents the difficulties associated with arranging extra meetings. It also can provide for broader representation of governor involvement rather than leaving it just to the chair and head. If decisions are delegated, either to a subcommittee or to the chair and head, they must be reported to the whole governing body, while keeping the names of the pupil(s) concerned confidential.

Situations may arise where the governing body as a whole needs to be involved anyway, and this will be better if it is sooner rather than later. This might be in circumstances when the LEA decides it needs to consult the governing body as a prerequisite to any action it may wish to take, or where a parent makes representations to the governing body or to the LEA about any kind of exclusion. The LEA may require the governing body to consider the parents' views before deciding on its next course of action.

Every governor also needs to be aware that they may not vote, or must withdraw from a meeting, if they have any direct or indirect connection with a disciplinary case that is being discussed. For example:

1. If a governor is a parent of a pupil whose discipline case is being considered, or whose child is involved in some way; or

2. If he or she had made allegations, and/or witnessed an incident about which disciplinary action against a pupil is being considered.

Record-keeping

This is essential. All pupils will have a personal file at school within which relevant and required information is kept about their progress. However, a systematic recording system of incidents which relate to any instances of misbehaviour should be an integral part of a discipline policy. If an exclusion and appeal situation does arise, accurate records will be needed. The facts are more likely to be accurate if accounts of incidents are recorded as soon as possible after they occur. While the detail of such arrangements is the responsibility of the headteacher, governors can expect accurate and comprehensive records to be kept. The following information is likely to be required.

Pupil's name

Pupil's date of birth

Date and time of incident

Description of incident

Names of any witnesses

Details of action taken

Note of relevant previous incidents

In relation to exclusions there will be a need to record:

Type of exclusion and, if appropriate, specific length;

Aggregate number of days the pupil has been excluded in the current term;

Details of who was informed of the exclusion and when.

LEAs may require gender and ethnic categories for monitoring purposes. Governors may also want to keep a record of this information in their schools.

It is very important that all issues relating to pupil indiscipline and related punishments are kept confidential. Schools have their own methods and systems of ensuring that such information is only accessible to a minimum number of, for example, named people. Governors should assure themselves that record-keeping is carried out in an appropriate way and includes only factual evidence of situations that have occurred, rather than examples of hearsay. They must also respect the need for confidentiality in any involvement they have with exclusion matters. As members of a legally constituted body they have access to information which would not otherwise be available to them. This access to confidential information must be respected.

Chapter 8

Exclusion and reinstatement appeals

Key points

- Involvement of governors
- The process
- Reinstatement issues

Local Education Authorities must make arrangements for pupils who are aged 18 or over, or for the parents/guardians of pupils who are under 18, to appeal against a permanent exclusion. Arrangements for appeals must also be made for governing bodies in situations where they do not agree with a decision made by the LEA, when the head has been directed by the LEA to reinstate a pupil who has been permanently excluded.

When a pupil is 18 or over he or she is informed directly in all the stages of the exclusion process, not through his or her parents.

In aided and special arrangement schools:

Only the governing body has the power to direct that a pupil who has been permanently excluded should be reinstated, and

Appeal committees are set up by the governing body.

Involvement of governors

This will depend on the circumstances of each appeal, and may not involve governors directly at all. For example, if the governors support the head in making an exclusion permanent, the parents have a right of appeal against the LEA. In this situation the parents would present an appeal (the appellants) against the LEA (the respondents). The governors, the third party, could be called to make representations to the appeals panel either in writing or in person. If this is not requested there is no requirement for them to be involved.

If the LEA directs the reinstatement of a pupil the governors can appeal against the LEA. In this situation the governors are the appellants, and the LEA the respondents. The parents, the third party, could be asked for their views and, as above, this can be done either in writing or in person.

Once a pupil has been permanently excluded from a school his or her name must be removed from the register. It is then the responsibility of the LEA to provide education in an appropriate environment. Governors no longer have a responsibility for that pupil. However, they may want to assure themselves that appropriate action is taken as quickly as possible to help the pupil, rather than 'washing their hands' of a major and resource-intensive problem.

The process

The framework for the process is contained within the *Education (No. 2) Act 1986*. A *Code of Practice*, relating particularly to the conduct of exclusion and reinstatement appeals was produced by the Local Authority Associations and others. It sets out guidelines within the legal requirements to try to ensure that correct and democratic procedures are followed. It was the subject of detailed consultation with the Council of Tribunals, and also involved representatives of church schools, other voluntary bodies, and the Department of Education and Science (DES).

This *Code of Practice* will have influenced the local appeals procedures produced by LEAs. (Copies of LEA appeals procedures should be readily available to parents and governors.) They deal with the formal situation and governors have a restricted role within them. Prior to the

governors may decide for themselves how they deal with exclusions in
their own context. The details of the appeals procedure should not vary
widely from LEA to LEA because of the guidance provided in the
Code of Practice. Appendix 2 contains notes of guidance for parents
about exclusion and reinstatement appeals, which is reproduced by
permission of Bedfordshire County Council. This document follows the
guidance contained in the *Code of Practice*, and also is reproduced in
community languages in accordance with the authority's equal opportunities policy.

The following notes provide a simplified version of the stages of the
process and the actions which must or may be taken by different parties
at different times.

What happens after an exclusion?

Short fixed period exclusion

Less than five days aggregate in any one term. No lack of opportunity
to take public examination.

Head *must* inform pupil's parents of exclusion period, reasons, and
their right to make representations to governing body and the LEA.

Parents *may* make representations

Governors Not normally involved. If parents make representation to
them or to LEA they may consider whether to modify the exclusion
period or not.

The reality is that the exclusion will probably have passed before it is
possible for them to take action, but all exclusions should be reported
to governors who would need to know whether the school's behaviour
policy is effective.

Fixed period exclusion

More than five days aggregate in any one term or loss of opportunity
to take examination: any such exclusion must be reported to governors.

Indefinite or permanent exclusion

Head *must* inform parents of exclusion period, type, reasons and right to make representations to governors and LEA.
Must inform governors and LEA of this too.

Parents *may* make representations.

Governors *may* decide to reinstate immediately, reinstate by a particular date or not to reinstate after own consideration, representations from parents or consultation with LEA. At least three governors must decide whether an excluded pupil should be reinstated; none of them should be the Head (Regulation 26(6)

LEA *must* decide after consultation with governors to:
Immediately, reinstate by a particular date or not to reinstate.
If reinstate, *must direct* head.
If not reinstate, *must* inform parents.

Head *must* comply with directions from governing body, or LEA. If directions are contradictory, whichever direction will lead to the earliest reinstatement of the pupil must be followed, *unless* head decides exclusion should be made permanent. (The process will repeat itself up to the direction stage.)

Parents *may* appeal against LEA's decision or head's decision that exclusion is made permanent.

Governors *may* appeal against LEA direction to reinstate a pupil who they had decided should be permanently excluded.

Reinstatement issues

If the governors decide to appeal against a reinstatement, they must do so in writing, setting out the reasons for the appeal, and within seven days of the LEA's notice directing the head to reinstate the pupil. This information is contained in Appendix 2 referred to above.

Appeals procedures are unpleasant for everyone. The parties involved are in conflict and the outcome will produce a winner and loser. Winning an appeal can sometimes give rise to other difficulties. For example, a decision to reinstate a pupil may result in strong feelings of resentment by teachers who may have been physically and/or verbally abused by the child, who may have tried to work with him/her and ultimately found that establishing a constructive relationship impossible. Governors need to be aware of the possible and/or likely effects, within the school, of a decision to reinstate, and if reinstatement is agreed to be assured that a planned programme of counselling will be provided for the pupil. Affected teachers may also need support.

The effective management of pupil reinstatement does not just apply to a discipline situation that has reached the appeal stage. Whatever the outcome of an appeal relationships are likely to be damaged between some or all of the parties involved. This fact should not be paramount in the deliberations: the best interests of the pupil should come first. The framework that has been established for the hearing of appeals goes some way to ensuring fairness and consistency in this process.

Chapter 9
Conclusion

The arrangements concerning disciplinary issues in schools brought in by the 1986 Act provide a fairer and more democratic approach to dealing with pupil behaviour which is deemed to be totally unacceptable. It is not always easy consistently to follow laid down guidelines and procedures when trying to effectively manage individual disciplinary problems. Every person is different, and therefore has different needs and requirements. However, the legislation does at least provide a framework within which certain rules must be followed in relation to exclusion, the most serious form of punishment. This goes some way towards reducing many of the extremes which previously existed before about how exclusions were handled.

Pupil discipline and exclusions are inextricably linked, and some of the key points for governors raised in the previous chapters are summarised below:

Governors need to have knowledge and awareness of:

How disciplinary issues are managed within the school, and who has responsibilities for different aspects of these;

Their own arrangements for handling discipline cases, who is involved and at what stage;

How school discipline features in the school development plan;

Communication arrangements between parents, the school and the wider community;

Their specific responsibilities in law which relate to the process of excluding a pupil;

Their responsibilities in law which relate to the internal disciplinary arrangements of the school.

Policies and procedures are important because they provide a framework within which everyone can try to operate consistently, and to which they can refer when needed. There is a danger, though, that once produced they are put away and brought out only when a problem arises. Governors will not need to refer to these documents in the same way as teachers will, but they should know how the discipline policies are put into action. They should also be sure that these policies are reviewed regularly so that they continue to meet the changing needs and requirements of the world at large. The detailed arrangements are the concern of the teachers. Ensuring the effectiveness of those arrangements is one of the important responsibilities of governors. They should not underestimate the contribution they can make to a planned and coordinated approach to dealing with school discipline issues.

There is concern in society about the continuing existence of different sorts of abuse that affect children. Some are battered and abused in ways which are illegal. Other are battered or abused in ways which are not illegal: this can include being on the receiving end of sarcastic, patronising and sexist remarks. The damaging effect of this type of abuse on some children often is not realised.

The abolition of corporal punishment has meant the end in schools of one abuse which many observed, heard about or suffered — or sometimes seemed to enjoy in a boastful way. Exclusions will be regarded by many as a more humane way of dealing with serious breaches of school discipline, especially if the exclusions are short-term. Exclusions are an extreme sanction within the total framework of school discipline. Even short ones can affect the learning process and a pupil's future. Indefinite or permanent exclusions, which used to be called expulsions, may have a significant effect on a pupil's school, later life and career. This is why any exclusion must be considered objectively and fairly.

It might always be reasonable for Governors to ask the question — is there another way?

In the case studies that follow the reader may feel that sometimes there was and sometimes there was not a more effective way of dealing with the incidents described. However, most governors will never be in the position of headteachers, teachers or others who have the responsibility of maintaining discipline, sometimes in very threatening situations. Sometimes, like jurors faced with conflicting evidence, governors may need to consider, and in their case ask questions about: procedures followed; courses of action considered; and alternative ways of dealing with cases. The judgement of governors must be as objective as possible and take into account the views of all concerned parties.

Chapter 10

Case studies

Introduction

This chapter contains six case studies which provide examples of exclusion and discipline situations. Each is based on reality, although the names of the people and places used are fictional. The notes are quite detailed in order to try and explain the complexities involved.

As you read them, try to do the following:

1. Imagine yourself in the situation described and decide whether you think that what actually happened was handled properly. If not, decide what you think could or should have been done differently.

2. If such a situation were to arise in your own school, decide whether or not you are confident that the necessary and appropriate systems and procedures are in place to deal with such events.

3. Do you think that the outcomes were in the best interests of the pupils?

It is important to remember that these examples are inevitably taken out of the environment in which they actually occurred, but reading them dispassionately should enable a greater degree of objectivity on the part of the reader. This point is worth remembering should you be called in at any stage of disciplinary proceedings. Comments on the cases are given at the end of the chapter.

Case studies

Case study 1

Harri is 11 years old and in his first term at Greenacres, a mixed 11–16 comprehensive school. Before he came to the school the headteacher had met with Harri's mother as well as with the liaison teacher in his primary school. Harri had been disruptive while at primary school, name-calling other pupils and with a tendency to violent behaviour. The educational psychologist was already involved and Harri had been considered for a place at a special school but his mother wanted him to have a chance at Greenacres. It was agreed that he would come to Greenacres, and would have regular counselling sessions with the deputy headteacher who had responsibility for pastoral work in the school.

A week before half-term he was seen by teachers between lessons kicking pupils. He said he was just playing. Two days after half-term Harri was seen hitting another pupil at break time. The headteacher asked to see him. The education welfare officer was also present. He was excluded for three days because of his aggressive behaviour.

He returned to school at the agreed time, and two weeks later was involved in similar incidents. Harri's parents were asked to come to school and talk about their son's behaviour which his mother agreed to do.

While he was removed from lessons he was given work to do and supervised by a member of staff. He continued to behave in a similarly violent way during lunch time, when his supervision was less strict.

A week later he returned to lessons but was involved in a further incident of hitting and kicking other pupils at break. At lunchtime he kicked another pupil in the ribs, which resulted in that pupil having to have a precautionary X-ray. As a result of this he was seen by the headteacher. Harri showed no remorse for his behaviour and was given a five-day exclusion. The day that he returned to school he was seen by a teacher to hit two more pupils, and was removed from lessons pending a decision on what action should be taken. At lunchtime he failed to follow an instruction from the head of year to stop bumping into other children. Later a prefect reported that a pupil had complained about being kicked. The head teacher decided to exclude him permanently from the school and this decision was supported by Harri's mother and by the chair of governors.

Case study 2

Neil is a 15 year-old boy in a mixed 11–18 high school. Although not one of the brightest pupils he tries hard, and generally manages to achieve average grades in his work. He comes from a family supportive to his educational progress and had never had any significant problems over discipline. However, in the first term of his fifth year (Y11) he became more introspective and moody. One morning just before break he was told off by a teacher for dropping paper on the floor, and was asked to pick it up and put it in the waste bin. Neil lost his temper, stalked out of the class room, and five minutes later was seen by the headteacher poking holes with an umbrella in the ceiling of one of the main corridors.

The headteacher called him into her study and asked for an explanation. Neil was very upset by what had happened and was ashamed of his behaviour. He told her that he had lost his temper because he did not like being told off by the teacher, and 'in a fit of pique took it out on the ceiling'.

The chair of the governors was in the school when this incident happened, saw the damage and heard firsthand information about Neil. The headteacher said that she was going to impose a two-day exclusion on Neil because of the damage to school property. The chair of governors queried this. He thought this punishment was too severe in view of Neil's obvious regret and previous good record.

Neil was removed from classes while a decision was made about further action that needed to be taken. His parents came to the school where the headteacher explained what had happened, and they went to talk with Neil. They returned to the headteacher's study saying that Neil was very upset and ashamed of what he had done. He admitted he had lost his temper, he was feeling generally low at the moment, he knew he had done wrong and had offered to pay for the cost of the damage he had caused. They did not feel that an exclusion on top of this would serve any useful purpose.

The headteacher decided that Neil should be excluded for two days, and that he should pay for the cost of the repairs over an agreed period of time. He had no further disciplinary problems during his time at school.

Case study 3

Martin and Clive were pupils at a mixed comprehensive school. They were both lively and outgoing and had no record of discipline problems. They were both 14 years old at the time of this incident.

One Friday they were both reprimanded for bad behaviour by their teacher and were taken from the classroom into the school office by the teacher. Both of them were said to be abusive to the teacher.

At lunchtime the incident was reported by the teacher to the headteacher.

After lunch Martin returned to school with his mother, who claimed that Martin had been struck by the teacher in the school office, and this had been witnessed by Clive. Martin had a bruise on his face.

The teacher accused was interviewed by the headteacher in the presence of the deputy headteacher. Both were satisfied that the teacher had not struck Martin and accepted the teacher's explanation that the bruising had been caused by a fall in the corridor after the lesson, and this was explained to his mother. The situation seemed to have been amicably resolved.

About twenty minutes after the end of the school day Martin returned to school with his older brother, Mark. They found the teacher in the school corridor and, according to the teacher, they hit him. Afterwards the teacher was seen to have a cut lip and black eye. The incident described by the teacher was confirmed by another member of the teaching staff and by the site manager.

On the following Monday this assault was investigated by the headteacher. Both parents were invited to the school to discuss the matter. The parents said that Martin had been hit by the teacher. The headteacher said that he thought that this matter had been satisfactorily resolved, and that the reason for this meeting was because one of his teachers had been hit by Martin and his brother. He was not prepared to tolerate assaults on members of his staff and would be excluding Martin for an indefinite period. On the Wednesday Martin's parents were informed that their son was to be permanently excluded from school because of the assault. The chair of governors received this information by letter on the same day.

On the following Friday the headteacher received a letter from the chair of governors protesting about the permanent exclusion and claiming that the alleged assault by the teacher on Martin had not been properly investigated. A second letter was received from the chair of governors the following week stating that a governors' subcommittee would meet to consider the matter. The parents were invited to a meeting with the chair of governors and one other governor.

Two weeks later this meeting took place. Full details were explained to the governors by the parents and a detailed written statement was submitted by them. They stressed that there had been a previous history of problems between Martin's older brothers, Martin and the teacher concerned. They admitted that it seemed that Martin had been abusive to the teacher but stressed that it was entirely unacceptable for the teacher to strike their son.

On the same day the headteacher and the teacher met with a senior officer of the LEA. Full details of the events were explained and the teacher again denied the alleged assault on Martin. Martin's parents were invited to visit the education office to discuss the incident with the senior education officer and the principal education welfare officer.

On the following Monday the governors' subcommittee met again to consider written statements of events submitted by the headteacher, the teacher and the parents. The governors reported to a special meeting of the full governing body two days later, when the permanent exclusion was confirmed. The LEA agreed with the decision.

After the parents had been informed of this they informed the education office of their wish to appeal against the decision. An appeal form was sent to the parents for completion.

The appeal took place at the education office one month later. Martin's parents, Martin, Mark and Clive appeared as witnesses. The education officer and headteacher appeared for the authority. The appeals committee consisted of three elected members, with a representative from the county secretary's department to provide legal advice and guidance. The decision of the appeals panel was that Martin should be reinstated at the school the following term. They stated that the assault on the teacher deserved punishment but due to 'the circumstances of the case as presented to them . . . permanent exclusion was not the appropriate response to the situation'. Meanwhile home tutorship should be provided.

The parents, having won their appeal, agreed to seek an alternative school for Martin.

Case study 4

Elizabeth is a 14 year-old pupil. She was given two detentions within two weeks, one for being rude to a member of staff and the other for disobeying instructions. It then came to light that she had not delivered the two detention letters to her mother. As a result she was given a two-day exclusion.

Four months later, during which time she had not caused any trouble, she was found writing obscene words on toilet walls during lesson time. She was told to clean off the graffiti, which she did. Her mother was contacted and Elizabeth was given a two-day exclusion. Four months after this incident Elizabeth started to be consistently rude in class to her mathematics teacher. Procedures laid down within the school's pastoral code of practice had been followed throughout this case, and when the deputy headteacher (pastoral affairs) became involved, she refused to follow his instructions. Again her mother was contacted and after discussion with her and her daughter, Elizabeth was given a three-day exclusion. Her inconsistent behaviour was giving serious cause for concern by teachers, and by this time the educational psychology service had been contacted for advice and reports. At this stage she seemed to quieten down and, although not always cooperative with teachers, her behaviour was described as manageable.

Seven months later she set fire to waste paper in two bins, one in a toilet and one in a cloakroom. No serious damage was done and no one was hurt. At this stage she was given an indefinite exclusion pending discussion with the chair of governors and the local education authority. During discussions Elizabeth indicated to the headteacher that she was likely to repeat this action.

She was permanently excluded from the school.

Case study 5

Mary is 15 and during her earlier years of secondary school, particularly in her second year showed signs of difficulty in accepting school discipline and adult authority. She was counselled about this, then started truanting from school. The education welfare officer was contacted immediately and she began to work with Mary and her family to try to get her to attend school. Her attendance soon improved but in the early part of her fourth year (Y10) she was involved in a series of incidents.

She was found stealing money from another pupil's bag, truanting from lessons again and writing graffiti in the classroom. Her parents were contacted and Mary was given a three-day exclusion. She seemed to settle down after this, but seven months later she swore at a teacher. Again her parents were contacted and she was given a one-day exclusion.

During the following year she was generally uncooperative, and frequently rude to staff and pupils. Absence from school became a problem yet again and by the beginning of the next school year this became a major problem. The education welfare officer increased the amount of time she spent with Mary to try and improve the situation. While the education welfare officer worked with Mary she usually attended school, but when this support was reduced she almost immediately absented herself again. The governors were aware of the situation and they and the staff were concerned about Mary's inability to conform.

Case study 6

Andrew started school when he was five years old. He did not settle well, and his parents were concerned and upset about the extent to which he appeared to be teased and called racist names by other pupils. At the end of his second term at the school they decided to move him as he seemed very unhappy.

He started at a different infant school the following term, and although described by his teacher as a bright child, he had difficulty in relating to both adults and children. In the classroom he took a long time to settle down to work, ignoring instructions given by his teacher, pulling faces and pushing other pupils' work on to the floor. In play he was inclined to be aggressive, sometimes kicking other children and throwing stones.

The headteacher and staff became very concerned about his antisocial behaviour and the head decided that the best course of action at that stage would be to ask for advice from the school educational psychology service. She explained to his parents the process that would be involved, including the need for them to sign a form of agreement. The parents were reluctant to cooperate. They seemed suspicious of the involvement of an outside service and unclear as to the purpose of any reports that might be written about Andrew. They appeared to have difficulty in communicating with the headteacher and were distrustful of her.

Eventually, however, they did agree, but relationships between them and the head became very strained.

Andrew was observed by a member of the LEA's pupil support services unit. This resulted in three hours' individual help each day being provided for him. Initially his behaviour improved. When given instructions on a one-to-one basis he was able to carry out tasks, and sometimes produced good work. However, his ability to work and play with other children did not show much improvement.

After a few weeks he again started to challenge adult authority, ignoring instructions and being very rude. He was excluded for two days. He returned to school on the agreed day but his behaviour towards other pupils became more violent, and he was seen knocking over smaller children. He also refused to follow rules of both playground and classroom games. One morning, in the playground, he hurled a stone at another child causing a cut which needed several stitches.

After this stone-throwing incident the headteacher decided that she could no longer guarantee the safety of other children while Andrew was in the school. The additional individual help given to him seemed to have had little effect and she believed that his achievements were limited by his behaviour difficulties.

During the last week of the term the headteacher excluded Andrew for five days, which were the two remaining days of the summer term, and the first three days of the following term, which would start in September. A letter was sent to his parents stating that he should not attend for the first three days of the next term while decisions were made about his future. He turned up at school on the first day of the autumn term and his parents were told to take him home because of the exclusion. After this the headteacher decided that he should be permanently excluded.

Andrew's parents did not want him to have yet another change so early in his school life. They eventually decided to appeal against the permanent exclusion. Appeal proceedings were started, but dropped when Andrew's parents were persuaded by the LEA to send their son to another school.

Comments on case studies

Case study 1

These notes are a very reduced summary of the details of this case. It illustrates the importance of accurate record keeping in order to try and represent as fair a picture as possible of events over a period of time. The school disciplinary procedures were followed by the pastoral team. The governors were not involved until the first exclusion except through the governors' subcommittee on pastoral affairs which kept a watching brief on all school disciplinary matters. The chair of governors was informed by the headteacher, both orally and in writing of the first exclusion and in writing of all the others. The situation was discussed with the headteacher when permanent exclusion was being considered. The chair of governors agreed with the recommendations of the head-teacher at each stage. These were confirmed by the whole governing body.

Harri was counselled in the school and received support from the educational psychology service. His mother was as cooperative as she could be but had difficulty in coping with a large young family on her own. Although she agreed to come to the school to talk about Harri's problems, she frequently failed to turn up. Home visits were not made by any members of the school staff.

After Harri had been permanently excluded he went to a special school. Before he left his junior school the educational psychologist had been trying to negotiate a placement for him in such a school even though his mother did not want this. At the time there were no places available. He did not settle at Greenacres. His permanent exclusion may have accelerated the process of finding him a place in the special school he now attends.

Case study 2

Although Neil had no previous history of disruptive behaviour the headteacher felt that he should be excluded because of the seriousness of the offence, in this case damage to another person's property. She also considered that Neil's punishment should be a deterrent to other pupils. The chair of the governors felt that in this particular instance Neil had suffered enough, and that excluding him would not help him and could even have the opposite effect. However, he did agree to support the headteacher in her final decision. She was quite clear about what she considered to be the appropriate punishment. The Discipline and Exclusions Policy of this school did contain statements which supported the headteacher's decision. The chair of governors seemed less clear about the content of the policy document and arguably more concerned about Neil as a person. This raises the potential dilemma about consistency, fairness and individual needs.

Case study 3

It is possible that this conclusion could have been reached by discussion with the headteacher and the parents without having to go through the appeals procedure, but in the event Martin emerged without the tarnish of a permanent exclusion.

The appeal itself was brought by the parents against the LEA. An education officer presented the case for the LEA and called the headteacher as witness. The parents called both their sons and Clive as witnesses. The only people who were present throughout the appeal, in addition to the appeal committee and LEA legal adviser, were the education officer and the parents. The teacher who was directly involved was not brought as a witness. Whether this would have strengthened the LEA's case and resulted in a different outcome cannot be known.

The governors were neither asked, nor chose to present information to the appeals panel, and were, therefore, not involved. They decided not to appeal against the decision. Two other technical points should also be considered.

The panel consisted of three elected members of the authority. *The Code of Practice for education appeals committees: exclusion and reinstatement appeals* discussed earlier, drawing on *Schedule 2 Para 1(4) of the Education Act 1980* states that: 'members of the appeals committee who are members of the authority or of any education committee shall not outnumber the others by more than one'. There were 'no others' – people with experience in education, uninvolved teachers or parents – on this panel.

The code also states that appeals 'ideally . . . should not be held in education department premises'.

Case study 4

This case illustrates a situation where a pupil is not consistently misbehaving, but over a period of time exhibits behaviour which contravened the school's expectations of reasonableness, and in the end, safety to others on the premises. The psychologist indicated that Elizabeth had difficulty in relating to males, as an effect of earlier childhood experiences. Her mother was contacted by the school and involved in discussions about her daughter from the start of observed difficulties. The pastoral team worked hard with her, and felt that some progress had been made in spite of her erratic behaviour. The headteacher's view was that he and his staff could do no more because she required an intensity of resources that they could not provide, and which would be at the cost of the many other pupils in the school. The governors were not involved in any discussions or reports about this case. The chair of governors was informed of the exclusions when they occurred and the action of the headteacher was endorsed by her and then reported to the next meeting of the governors. There was no discussion about any other solution, such as an appeal or reinstatement.

Case study 5

Mary's problems took place over a period of 18 months. She remained on the school register, and was provided with extra support to try to improve her attendance record and help her with her related learning problems.

The pastoral team set up a special working party, including some governors, to review their methods and procedures for communicating with parents on discipline issues. This was initiated partly because of Mary's case. The matter is still unresolved.

Case study 6

Andrew had an unfortunate start to his school life. Poor communication seems to have been part of the problem with misunderstandings and suspicion between his parents and the headteacher. Poor interpersonal communication was only part of the problem. The governors were not informed or involved in this case at any stage until Andrew was excluded for five days, at the very end of the school term. The head-teacher did not tell his parents of their right to appeal or make representations to the governors or the LEA. They were later told this by the LEA. It is difficult to understand what benefit there would have been to Andrew by excluding him for five days over a period of eight weeks, with the summer holiday in between. Insensitivity and ignorance have played a part in hindering and probably damaging his early development. Legislation now exists to try and stop or minimise such incidents. Procedures at the school have now been examined by the governors, the LEA and the staff.

Appendix 1

Education (No 2) Act 1986 c. 61 Part III

Discipline

General duties

22. The articles of government for every county, voluntary and maintained special school shall provide—

    (*a*) for it to be the duty of the head teacher to determine measures (which may include the making of rules and provision for enforcing them) to be taken with a view to—

        (i) promoting, among pupils, self-discipline and proper regard for authority;
        (ii) encouraging good behaviour on the part of pupils;
        (iii) securing that the standard of behaviour of pupils is acceptable; and
        (iv) otherwise regulating the conduct of pupils;

    (*b*) for it to be the duty of the head teacher, in determining any such measures—

        (i) to act in accordance with any written statement of general principles provided for him by the governing body; and

(ii) to have regard to any guidance that they may offer in relation to particular matters;

(c) for it to be the duty of the head teacher to make any such measures generally known within the school;

(d) for the standard of behaviour which is to be regarded as acceptable at the school to be determined by the head teacher, so far as it is not determined by the governing body;

(e) for it to be the duty of the governing body and the head teacher to consult the local education authority, before determining any such measures, on any matter arising from the proposed measures which can reasonably be expected —

(i) to lead to increased expenditure by the authority; or
(ii) to affect the responsibilities of the authority as an employer;

(f) for the power to exclude a pupil from the school (whether by suspension, expulsion or otherwise) to be exercisable only by the head teacher.

Exclusion of pupils: duty to inform parents etc.

23. The articles of government for every county, voluntary and maintained special school shall provide—

(a) for it to be the duty of the head teacher —

(i) where he excludes from the school a pupil who is under eighteen, to take (without delay) reasonable steps to inform a parent of the pupil of the period of the exclusion and the reasons for it;

(ii) where he decides that any exclusion of such a pupil from the school which was originally for a fixed or indefinite period should be made permanent, to take (without delay) reasonable steps to inform a parent of the pupil of his decision and of the reasons for it; and

(iii) where he excludes any pupil from the school to take (without delay) reasonable steps to inform the pupil, if he is aged eighteen or over, or a parent of his, if he is under eighteen, that the pupil or (as the case may be) parent may make representations about the exclusion to the governing body and the local education authority;

(b) for it to be the duty of the head teacher, where he excludes a pupil from the school—

(i) for more than five school days (in the aggregate) in any one term; or

(ii) in circumstances in which the pupil would, as a result of his exclusion from the school, lose an opportunity to take any public examination;

to inform the local education authority and the governing body (without delay) of the period of the exclusion and of the reasons for it and where he decides that any exclusion of a pupil from the school which was originally for a fixed or indefinite period should be made permanent, to inform them (without delay) of his decision and of the reasons for it.

Reinstatement of excluded pupils: county, controlled and maintained special schools

24. The articles of government for every county, controlled and maintained special school shall provide—

(a) for it to be the duty of the local education authority, where they have been informed of the permanent exclusion of a pupil from the school—

(i) to consider, after consulting the governing body, whether he should be reinstated immediately, reinstated by a particular date or not reinstated;

(ii) where they consider that he should be reinstated, to give the appropriate direction to the head teacher; and

(iii) where they consider that he should not be reinstated, to inform the pupil (if he is aged eighteen or over) or a parent of his (if he is under eighteen) of their decision;

(b) for it to be the duty of the head teacher, where he has excluded a pupil from the school—

(i) for more than five school days (in the aggregate) in any one term; or

(ii) in circumstances in which the pupil would, as a result of his exclusion from the school, lose an opportunity to take any public examination;

to comply with any direction for the reinstatement of the pupil given by the governing body or the local education authority, in the case of an exclusion for a fixed period, or by the governing body, in the case of an exclusion which is for an indefinite period or is permanent;

(c) for it to be the duty of the local education authority, where they have been informed of the indefinite exclusion of a pupil from the school, to consult the governing body and, where the governing body do not intend to direct the head teacher to reinstate the pupil or the authority consider that he should be reinstated by a date which is earlier than that determined by the governing body as the date by which he is to be

reinstated— (i) to direct that he be reinstated immediately; or

(ii) to direct that he be reinstated within such period as may be specified in the direction;

(d) for it to be the duty of the local education authority where—

(i) they have been informed of the exclusion of a pupil from the school for a fixed period; and

(ii) they propose to give a direction for his reinstatement;

to consult the governing body before doing so;

(e) for any direction given by virtue of paragraph (c) above to cease to have effect (without prejudice to any subsequent direction given by virtue of any other provision made by the articles in accordance with this section) if the head teacher decides that the exclusion of the pupil concerned should be made permanent.

(f) for it to be the duty of the head teacher to comply with any direction given in exercise of the duty imposed on the local education authority by virtue of paragraph (*a*) or (*c*) above;

(*g*) for it to be the duty of the head teacher, where conflicting directions for the reinstatement of a pupil are given by the governing body and the local education authority, to comply with that direction which will lead to the earlier reinstatement of the pupil; and

(*h*) for it to be the duty of the governing body and the local education authority to inform each other and—

> (i) the pupil concerned, if he is aged eighteen or over; or
> (ii) a parent of his, if he is under eighteen;

of any direction, of a kind mentioned in this section, which is given by them.

Reinstatement of excluded pupils: aided and special agreement schools

25. The articles of government for every aided and special agreement school shall provide—

(*a*) for it to be the duty of the governing body, where they have been informed of the permanent exclusion of a pupil from the school—

> (i) to consider whether he should be reinstated immediately, reinstated by a particular date or not reinstated;
> (ii) where they consider that he should be reinstated, to give the appropriate direction to the head teacher; and
> (iii) where they consider that he should not be reinstated, to inform (without delay) the local education authority and either the pupil, if he is aged eighteen or over, or a parent of his, if he is under eighteen, of their decision;

(*b*) for it to be the duty of the head teacher where he has excluded a pupil from the school—

> (i) for more than five school days (in the aggregate) in any one term; or

      (ii) in circumstances in which the pupil would, as a result of his exclusion from the school, lose an opportunity to take any public examination;

to comply with any direction for the reintatement of the pupil given by the governing body or, in the case of an exclusion for a fixed period, by the governing body or the local education authority;

(c) for it to be the duty of the local education authority to consult the governing body before giving any direction by virtue of paragraph (b) above;

(d) for it to be the duty of the local education authority, where they have been informed of the indefinite exclusion of a pupil from the school, to consult the governing body and, where the governing body do not intend to direct the head teacher to reinstate the pupil or the authority consider that he should be reinstated by a date which is earlier than that determined by the governing body as the date by which he is to be reinstated—

      (i) to direct that he be reinstated immediately; or
      (ii) to direct that he be reinstated within such period as may be specified in the direction;

(e) for any direction given by virtue of paragraph (d) above to cease to have effect (without prejudice to any direction given by virtue of any other provision made by the articles in accordance with this section) if the head teacher decides that the exclusion of the pupil concerned should be made permanent;

(f) for it to be the duty of the head teacher to comply with any direction given in exercise of the duty imposed on the local education authority by virtue of paragraph (d) above;

(g) for it to be the duty of the head teacher, where conflicting directions for the reinstatement of a pupil are given by the governing body and the local education authority, to comply with that direction which will lead to the earlier reinstatement of the pupil; and

(*h*) for it to be the duty of the governing body and the local education authority to inform each other and—

(i) the pupil concerned, if he is aged eighteen or over; or

(ii) a parent of his, if he is under eighteen;

of any direction, of a kind mentioned in this section, which is given by them.

Appeals

26.—(1) Every local education authority shall make arrangements for enabling—

(*a*) a registered pupil at a county, controlled or maintained special school who is aged eighteen or over, or a parent of his, in the case of a pupil at such a school who is under eighteen, to appeal against any decision not to reinstate the pupil following his permanent exclusion from the school; and

(*b*) any governing body of such a school, the head teacher of which has been directed by the authority to reinstate any registered pupil at the school who has been permanently excluded, to appeal against the direction.

(2) The governing body of every aided or special agreement school shall make arrangements for enabling a registered pupil at the school who is aged eighteen or over, or a parent of a pupil at such a school who is under eighteen to appeal against any decision not to reinstate the pupil following his permanent exclusion from the school.

(3) Joint arrangemens may be made under subsection (2) above by the governing bodies of two or more aided or special agreement schools maintained by the same local education authority.

(4) Any appeal by virtue of this section shall be to an appeal committee constituted in accordance with Part I of Schedule 2 to the 1980

Act; and Schedule 3 to this Act shall have effect, in place of Part II of Schedule 2 to the 1980 Act, in relation to any such appeal.

(5) The decision of an appeal committee on any such appeal shall be binding on the persons concerned; and where the committee determines that the pupil in question should be reinstated it shall direct that he be reinstated immediately or direct that he be reinstated by such date as is specified in the direction.

Exclusion: additional provision for appeals

27. Where the articles of government for any county, voluntary or maintained special school provide—

(a) for the parents of any pupil who is excluded from the school in circumstances in which no right of appeal is given by section 26 of this Act to have the right to appeal against his exclusion to a person specified by the articles; and

(b) for the procedure to be followed on such an appeal;

any decision on such an appeal that the pupil should be reinstated, or that he should be reinstated earlier than would otherwise be the case, shall be binding on the head teacher.

Local education authority's reserve power

28.—(1) Every local education authority shall have power, in the circumstances mentioned in subsection (3) below, to take such steps in relation to any county, controlled or special school maintained by them as they consider are required to prevent the breakdown, or continuing breakdown, of discipline at the school.

(2) The governing body and the head teacher of every aided and special agreement school shall, in the circumstances mentioned in subsection (3) below, consider any representations made to them by the local education authority.

(3) The circumstances are that—

(a) in the opinion of the authority—

(i) the behaviour of registered pupils at the school; or

(ii) any action taken by such pupils or their parents;

is such that the education of any such pupils is, or is likely in the immediate future to become, severely prejudiced; and

(b) the governing body have been informed in writing of the authority's opinion.

(4) Steps taken by an authority under subsection (1) above may include the giving of any direction to the governing body or head teacher.

Appendix 2

Bedfordshire County Council Education (No 2) Act 1986 Exclusion and reinstatement appeals

Notes of guidance for parents

Introduction

These notes have been prepared by Bedfordshire County Council. They describe and explain the procedure for making an application to an Appeals Committee and the way in which the Committee will operate.

The *Education (No 2) Act 1986* requires all Local Education Authorities to make arrangements for parents (or pupils themselves if they are over 18) to appeal against a decision not to reinstate a pupil following his/her *permanent* exclusion from school (Exclusion Appeals).

The school's governing body too has a right of appeal against a direction by the local education authority that a pupil, who has been permanently excluded shall be reinstated, and the pupil's parents may attend and make representations at such an appeal (Reinstatement Appeals).

A. Exclusion appeals

How do I appeal?

If you wish to appeal against the decision not to reinstate your child, you should complete the form of appeal attached to these notes and return it to the County Secretary by the date indicated on the form. *It is most important that you specify the grounds of your appeal and that you comply with the time limit for submitting an appeal.*

When will my appeal be heard?

The County Secretary will advise you of the date of the hearing, and, unless you agree otherwise, at least 14 days' notice will be given.

Appeal Hearings will normally take place during the day, although in exceptional circumstances they may be held in the evening.

Where will my appeal be heard?

Appeals will usually take place in Luton or Bedford as appropriate.

Who are the Appeals Committee?

The Appeals Committee will consist of three people selected as follows:
    one from a panel of Education Committee Members;
    one from a panel of other County Councillors;
    one from a panel of persons who are not Members of either the Education Committee or the County Council but who have experience in education.

Will I have an opportunity to attend the hearing and put my case?

You have a right to attend the hearing and make oral and/or written representations. If you wish, you may be accompanied or represented, by a friend, though legal representation will seldom be necessary or appropriate.

Do I have the right to call witnesses in support of my case?

You may wish to ask witnesses to give evidence at the hearing and to challenge the evidence put forward by the local education authority and the school's governing body. In such circumstances you should:
1. Indicate what witnesses you propose to call on your form of appeal.
2. Provide copies of reports prepared by the witnesses when you send your form of appeal or as soon as possible thereafter, but in any event, before the hearing of the appeal.

This information is required to enable the LEA to consider your case carefully. If you fail to comply with this request and produce evidence without warning at the hearing, it may be necessary for the hearing to be adjourned.

What if I decide not to attend the hearing?

If you are unable to attend the hearing you should advise the County Secretary (in writing if possible) of the reasons why before the hearing date. If you do not do so and fail to attend the hearing, or if you elect not to attend, a decision will be taken in your absence by the Appeals Committee on the information that is available.

Who else will attend?

Appeals will be heard in private. An officer of the LEA will attend to present the authority's case, and it is also possible that the school's governing body will be represented.

What procedure will be followed at the hearing?

The conduct of proceedings is at the discretion of the Appeals Committee. However, it is likely that the procedure will be as follows:

1. The LEA's representative will present the authority's case and will call any witnesses (e.g. the school's headteacher). The parent will have an opportunity to question the representative and any witnesses.
2. The parent presents his/her case and calls any witnesses. The LEA's representative may question the parent and any witnesses.
3. The governing body may make representations.
4. The LEA's representative makes final representations.
5. The parent makes final representations.
6. The Appeals Committee will then deliberate and reach a decision.

When will I know if my appeal has been successful?

You will be notified in writing of the Appeals Committee's decision and the grounds upon which it has been made. Every effort will be made to ensure that you receive the decision within a day or so of the hearing.

The decision of the Appeal's Committee is binding on the persons concerned, i.e. the LEA, the school's governing body, the parents and the pupil.

If the Appeals Committee decide to allow the appeal, they will specify the date upon which the pupil shall be reinstated.

B. Reinstatement appeals

If the LEA direct that a pupil, who has been permanently excluded, shall be reinstated, the governing body of the school may appeal against that decision to the Appeals Committee.

An appeal must be submitted within seven days of the governing body being notified of the LEA's direction. Notice of appeal must be in writing setting out the grounds upon which it is made.

The parents of the pupil (or the pupil himself/herself if over 18) may make representations either in writing or orally to the Appeals Committee.

The pupil's parents will be notified of the hearing date so that they can attend to make representations if they so wish. The procedure at the hearing will be as follows:

1. The LEA's representative will present the authority's case and will call any witnesses. The governing body's representative will be given an opportunity to put questions.
2. The governing body's representative will present the governing body's case and call any witnesses. The LEA's representative will be given an opportunity to put questions.
3. The parent may make representations. (Note: The parent has no right to call witnesses or to put questions to witnesses called by the LEA or the governing body.)
4. The LEA and governing body's representatives make final representations.
5. The Appeals Committee deliberate and reach their decision.

The Appeals Committee's decision and the grounds upon which it is made, will be notified in writing to the parent, governing body and LEA. The decision is binding on all concerned.

Bedfordshire County Council Permanent Exclusion Appeals

Form of appeal

If you wish to appeal against the Local education authority's decision not to reinstate your child, you should complete and return this form to:

The County Secretary,
Bedfordshire County Council,
County Hall
Bedford,
MK42 9AP

The form should be returned **as soon as possible and in any event before** ....

- -

I wish to appeal against the decision to exclude my child from school.

1. Full name of child
2. Child's date of birth
3. Name of school
4. Names of any witnesses you intend to call in support of your appeal

5. **Grounds of Appeal:** Please state your grounds of appeal overleaf continuing on a separate sheet if necessary.
6. Full name, address and   Name:
   day time telephone number of   Address:
   Parent/Guardian

                                              Telephone Number:

I understand that my appeal will be heard by an appeals committee which I have the right to attend.

Signed ....   Date ....

Note: Notification of the time, place and date of the hearing will be sent to you in due course. If you fail to attend the hearing, the appeal will be heard in your absence on the information that is available.

Grounds of appeal

Please continue on a separate sheet if necessary

Reproduced by kind permission of Bedfordshire County Council

References and further reading

Bedfordshire County Council 1990 *Bedfordshire High and Upper Schools: responses to difficult and disruptive behaviour 1988–89*

Elton, Lord 1989 *Discipline in schools: report on the committee of enquiry chaired by Lord Elton* HMSO

Education Act 1981 Section 2(5). HMSO 1981

Education (No 2) Act 1986 Sections 22–28. HMSO 1986

Mortimore P *et al. School matters: the junior years* Open Books 1988

Rosenbaum M 'Laying down the law' in *School Governor* September 1988

Tattum D, Herbert G 1990 *Bullying: a positive response* Cardiff SGIHE